LANGUAGE ARTS

Learning About

Poems

by Martha E. H. Rustad

Consulting Editor: Gail Saunders-Smith, PhD

Consultant: Kelly Boswell, educational consultant

CAPSTONE PRESS
a capstone imprint

Pebble Plus is published by Capstone Press,
1710 Roe Crest Drive, North Mankato, Minnesota 56003
www.capstonepub.com

Library of Congress Cataloging-in-Publication Data
Rustad, Martha E. H. (Martha Elizabeth Hillman), 1975–
  Learning about poems / Martha E. H. Rustad.
      pages cm—(Language arts)
  Includes bibliographical references and index.
  Includes webliography.
  ISBN 978-1-4914-0580-2 (hb)—ISBN 978-1-4914-0614-4 (eb)—ISBN 978-1-4914-0648-9 (pb)
1. Poetics—Juvenile literature. 2. Poetry—Authorshp—Juvenile literature. 3. Children's poetry, American. I. Title.
PN1042.R86 2014
  808.1—dc23   2014002015

Editorial Credits
Erika L. Shores, editor; Terri Poburka, designer; Charmaine Whitman, production specialist

Photo Credits
Shutterstock: Ahturner, 7, iofoto, 21, Karen Givens, 19 (dog), kesterhu, 19 (night sky), Legacy Images, 9, Levent Konuk, 11, luchschen, 17, Maxim Petrichuk, 5, Rob Marmion, 13, SNEHIT, 15, Szasz-Fabian Jozsef, cover (boy), topseller, cover (hot air balloon)

For Connie.—MEHR

Note to Parents and Teachers

The Language Arts set supports Common Core State Standards for Language Arts related to craft and structure, to text types and writing purpose, and to research for building and presenting knowledge. This book describes and illustrates poetry. The images support early readers in understanding the text. The repetition of words and phrases helps early readers learn new words. This book also introduces early readers to subject-specific vocabulary words, which are defined in the Glossary section. Early readers may need assistance to read some words and to use the Table of Contents, Glossary, Read More, Internet Sites, Critical Thinking Using the Common Core, and Index sections of the book.

Printed in the United States of America in North Mankato, Minnesota.
032014   008087CGF14

Table of Contents

What Is a Poem?

Poems connect words with senses
and feelings. Words in a poem
can make you feel warm
and happy. They can make
you feel silly or even sad.

Sunshine

by Laura Purdie Salas

Look for yellow
when you're weary

Smiling color
makes you cheery

Lemonade
in hot July

Flowers
reaching for the sky

Shining when
you need a lift

Nature's golden
brightest gift

A poet is someone who writes poems. Poets pick words carefully. In a poem, just a few words can tell us about a big idea.

Making Pancakes

by Laura Purdie Salas

pour the batter
Plip
Plop

brown both sides
Flip
Flop

spread the butter
Tip
Top

let the syrup
Drip
Drop

eat them all up
Don't
Stop!

Poem Parts

Poems are made up of lines
and stanzas. A line is all
the words in one row.
A stanza is a group of lines.

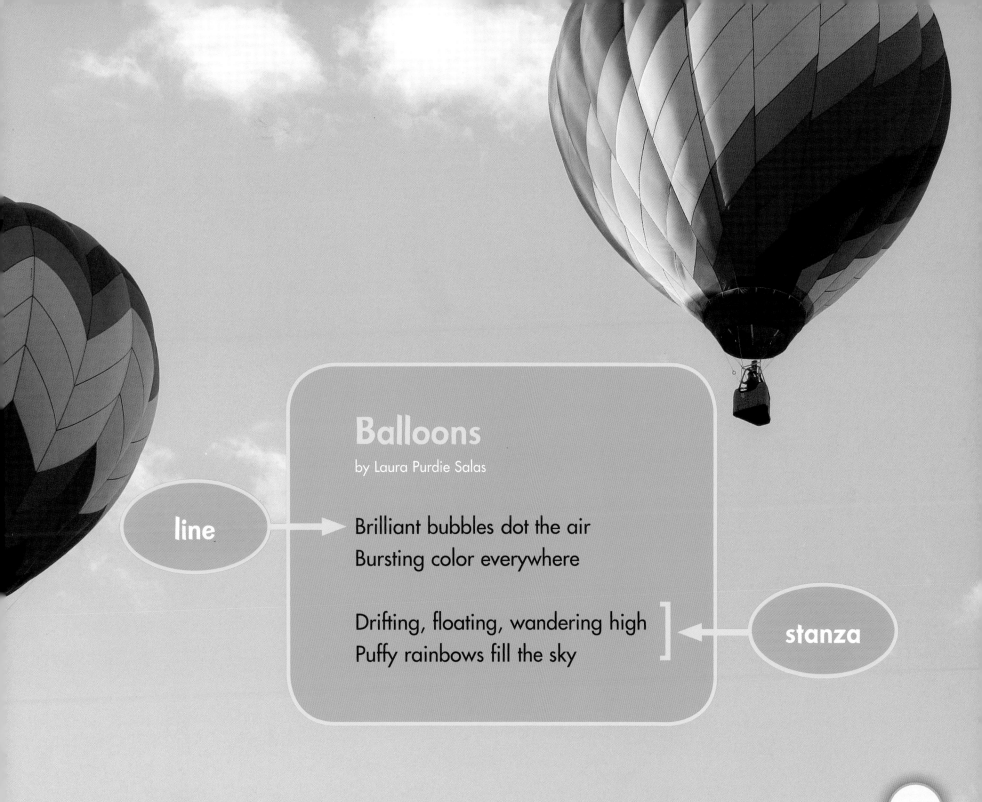

line

Balloons
by Laura Purdie Salas

Brilliant bubbles dot the air
Bursting color everywhere

Drifting, floating, wandering high
Puffy rainbows fill the sky

stanza

9

Some poems use words
that rhyme, or sound alike.
In this poem, "rye," "high,"
and "sky" rhyme.

Skyscraper Sandwich

by Laura Purdie Salas

I once built a sandwich on rye
Swiss cheese and bologna stretched high
It stood straight and tall
I did not let it fall
I stopped when my sandwich hit sky!

Rhythm is a pattern you hear

when you read words out loud.

Read the poem "Kick!" out loud.

Do you hear its steady rhythm?

Kick!

by Catherine Ipcizade

There once was a girl who could kick,
spent all of her days kicking sticks,
till she spotted a ball,
kicked it clear through a wall,
and began playing soccer right quick.

Some poems use one letter often.

This poem has a lot of S's.

Alliteration means using

the same letter often.

Snaking
by Laura Purdie Salas

Rivers
slither
through
like
snakes
stretching
in sun,
rippling
sleek
muscles

15

Some poems compare one thing

to something else. This poem

says snow covers things,

just like a blanket does.

The First Snowfall

by Jennifer Fandel

Hard, cold
rains lighten to
white, shimmering crystals.
Like a blanket, the snow covers
us. *Hush.*

Kinds of Poems

Words are made of syllables.
You hear a syllable as a loud or
soft sound. In haikus and cinquains
(SIN-kanes), each line has
a certain number of syllables.

A haiku has
5 syllables,
7 syllables, and
5 syllables.

Persieds

by Martha E. H. Rustad

Shining stars up high,
Quiet night, you on my lap.
Meteors rain down.

No Need to Shower When Your Pet's a St. Bernard

for Brutus, by Blake Hoena

He shakes
his massive head,
and gobs of slobber fly,
showering the walls, the TV,
and me.

A cinquain has
2 syllables,
4 syllables,
6 syllables,
8 syllables, and
2 syllables.

19

Can you write an acrostic poem?

In acrostic poems, the first letter

in each line spells something.

Use the letters in your name.

You are a poet!

Music flows
Apple sliced
Retell a story
Kiss a nose
Under starry sky
Settle down

21

Glossary

acrostic—a poem that spells a word with the first letter of each line

alliteration—using several words that start with the same letter sound

cinquain—a poem that has a certain number of syllables in each line; the first line has two syllables, the second has four, the third has six, the fourth has eight, and the last line has two syllables

haiku—a poem that has a certain number of syllables in each line; the first and third lines have five syllables, and the second line has seven

line—all the words in one row of a poem

poet—a person who writes poems

rhyme—similar sounds in words

rhythm—a regular, repeated pattern heard when words are read aloud

stanza—a group of lines

syllable—one part of sound in a word

Read More

Loewen, Nancy. *Words, Wit, and Wonder: Writing Your Own Poem.* Writer's Toolbox. Minneapolis: Picture Window Books, 2009.

McCurry, Kristen. *Pick a Picture, Write a Poem!* Little Scribe. North Mankato, Minn.: Capstone Press, 2014.

Nesbitt, Kenn. *The Tighty Whitey Spider: And More Wacky Animal Poems I Totally Made Up.* Naperville, Ill.: Sourcebooks Jabberwocky, 2010.

Internet Sites

FactHound offers a safe, fun way to find Internet sites related to this book. All of the sites on FactHound have been researched by our staff.

Here's all you do:

Visit *www.facthound.com*

Type in this code: 9781491405802

Super-cool stuff! Check out projects, games and lots more at **www.capstonekids.com**

Critical Thinking Using the Common Core

1. Some poems use alliteration. Describe what alliteration means. Try writing a poem that uses alliteration. (Craft and Structure)

2. Describe how you can tell if a poem is a haiku or a cinquain. (Key Ideas and Details)

Index

Word Count: 210 (main text)

Grade: 1

Early-Intervention Level: 18